# SIGN LANGUAGE

Caroline Fitton and her sister
showing an early interest in
sign language.

To my family—Woody, Duch, Nick, Moyd and O.D.—
and to Malcolm, Fay, Geoff and Jane, with
thanks for all their geo/graphic enthusiasm.

Caroline Fitton is a freelance editor
and researcher who pursues photography
in her spare time. Born in
Stoke-on-Trent, she now lives in
North London. This is her first book.

Index of locations on page 94

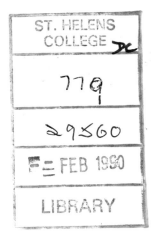

First published 1987 by
André Deutsch Limited
105-106 Great Russel Street
London WC1B 3LJ

Photographs © 1987 by Caroline Fitton
Introduction © 1987 by Tom Sharpe

Fitton, Caroline
Sign language.
1. Photography, Artistic 2. Photography by signs and signboards.
I. Title
779'.4'0924 TR659
ISBN 0-233-98164-0

Designed by Don Macpherson

Typeset by BH Graphics Ltd., 10 Aintree Road, Perivale, Middlesex.
Printed in England by Ebenezer Baylis & Son Ltd, Worcester and London.

# SIGN LANGUAGE

Caroline Fitton
Introduction by Tom Sharpe

ANDRÉ DEUTSCH

# INTRODUCTION

As an unpublished photographer of thirty years' standing, it naturally irks me to write this introduction. Any one who has gone through the routine of, at first, taking dozens of lousy photographs and then developing them so that the resulting prints look like something that a totally colour-blind child of two might have created with a bucket of black paint and glaringly white piece of paper, will know what I mean. We, the great unviewed, have gone through the purgatory of nights and days in makeshift darkrooms and have kept the shares of film, paper, developer and fixer manufacturers high and yielding remarkably decent dividends. We have also boosted both the German and of late the Japanese economies by our own purchases. In my case I can no longer count the number of cameras I have bought in the futile belief that equipment would turn me into a better Cartier Bresson, a Bill Brandt or even, in my madder moments, a lesser Ansel Adams. Had I invested the money I spent on these gadgets I would not now be forced by financial circumstances to be writing this introduction, but instead would be buying the book itself or ordering it from the Cayman Islands.

I mention these juvenile and, alas, maturer follies of mine only to establish some credentials. Thirty years is a long time to have spent in darkrooms mixing developers and, even in the days before selenium toner was available in the shops, concocting in the kitchen a deadly mixture of sodium sulphite anhydrous and the skin-absorbative and lethal selenium powder in a saucepan over a gas stove — all in the hope that my photographs would have archival quality and last five hundred years, or until the paper base cracked up. More, I have used every size of camera, from Leicas and Nikons through Rolleiflexes and Hasselblads to 8 x 10 Gandolfis and Kodaks, and have dedicated more reading hours to the study of the Zone System without understanding one word of it, than sensible people have spent trying to find the philosopher's stone and turn lead into gold. When I say that I have even sat at the feet of Paul Strand's enlargers and dipped my fingers in the D23 developer he used for his negatives, the aficionados of the camera (literally) obscura will realize my zeal. I have copied every technique under the sun and I have failed.

Contrast this with the achievements of Miss Fitton. She knew absolutely nothing (I have this from her own delightful lips) about developers, chloro-bromide papers, the merits of acetic acid and stop bath; she simply looked at the world around her with the eyes of an innocent into whose hands a rather cheap, and in my view nasty, camera happened to have landed. Worse still, from my point of view again, she travelled round the country doing exactly what I had done in 1967 — photographing signs, shop fronts, decrepit buildings and the strange assortment of items advertised in rather battered and down-at-heel shops. She did this without my hard-won expertise too. Dammit, she didn't bother with polarizing filters or cameras whose backs tilted and whose fronts rose and whose lenses she had tested time and time again. She didn't bother about converging verticals or depth of focus and stopping down to F64 like Edward Weston and all dedicated photographers on the Californian coast; and didn't even know that such things could be done or that the Zone System existed. She simply photographed what she saw and what took her interest. And, heresy beyond heresy, the wretch didn't even use transparency film which every honest photographer knows is the *sine qua non* of really good printing. SHE USED COLOUR NEGATIVE FILM and probably bought the stuff from the nearest chemist. It hadn't even been kept at the right temperature which, as everyone knows, is less than 55 degrees fahrenheit and only to be maintained in a fridge. Finally, and most damning of all, having taken her pictures (without bracketing the exposure, let me add) she then took the muck to Snippy Snaps or Four Minute Pics and had her shots back as enprints after lunch. Can I say more?

Unfortunately and grudgingly I have to. Miss Fitton has what I and my companions in a million darkrooms — those unsung (thank God) heroes with metol- or amidol-stained fingers who know about enlargers, the importance of stop baths and the temperature of the print wash water — have not got: an instinctive eye for the world about her. She is interested not in techniques but in the things that are there outside the camera obscura. Where we dodge about like demented dragonflies with light meters, she ignores everything that interferes with what she sees. She goes up to it, aims her camera and presses the button. Kodak or the local chemist do the rest.

But the rest is unimportant. The world she has recorded is that faded, shabby and strangely moving world of signs which recall a past when Ovaltinies ruled OK, or a present in which President Reagan's hearing aid may yet bring some customer through the door. Pathos paints the streets of Miss Fitton's Britain, a pathos born of contrast between the crumbling relics of nineteenth-century confidence and the aspirations of a hopeless generation that still strives and, for all I know, succeeds in making fortunes behind the shoddy, modern shop fronts. Whatever else the British may have lost, Miss Fitton's photographs deny us pessimism. Hope springs, until it is bulldozed, eternal in the back streets. Were I a semiotic expert, which I am glad to say I am not, I might write a thesis on the meaning of street signs. I would be wasting my time as effectively as I waste it in the darkroom. Miss Fitton's pictures say it all. Or almost all. One can laugh, one is in fact forced to laugh with her, at the continuing optimism of her images, or lament the decline of the inner cities and trace the shift in architectural styles from Victorian Solidity through the Odeonic Thirties to the Pompidouic Present; but one cannot escape the unbroken tradition of comic irony that seems always to have been the saving grace of British shopkeepers, no matter from what corner of the world they gathered. Behind the signs there are the anonymous craftsmen - even we of the darkroom. Miss Fitton's photographs celebrate the absurdity of our vision and make us laugh at the results of our own indomitable expertise.

*Tom Sharpe*

GAMES
&
VIEWING
LOUNGE
UPSTAIRS

'Worst band ever'
— the TIMES

'Music for Morons'
— the SUN

'Stoke's worst band'
— EVENING
SENTINEL

# the NUKES

16

CUTTY SARK Tall ships race

*July 15th – July 19th*
NEWCASTLE MARITIME FESTIVAL
*July 7th – July 27th*

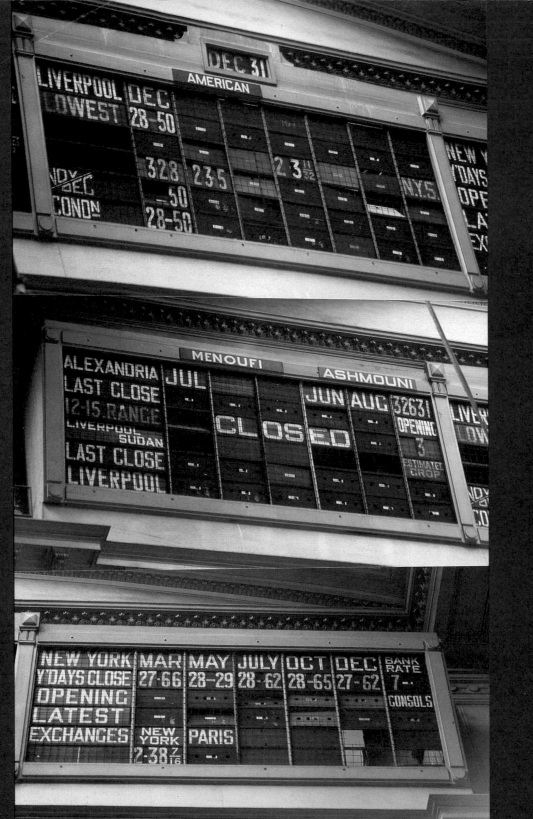

*Food for Thought*

44

*You don't have to be mad to drink here!*

HOURS OF
BUSINESS
MON-FRI :
8·30-5·30
SAT :
8·30-1·30

*When the boat comes in . . .*

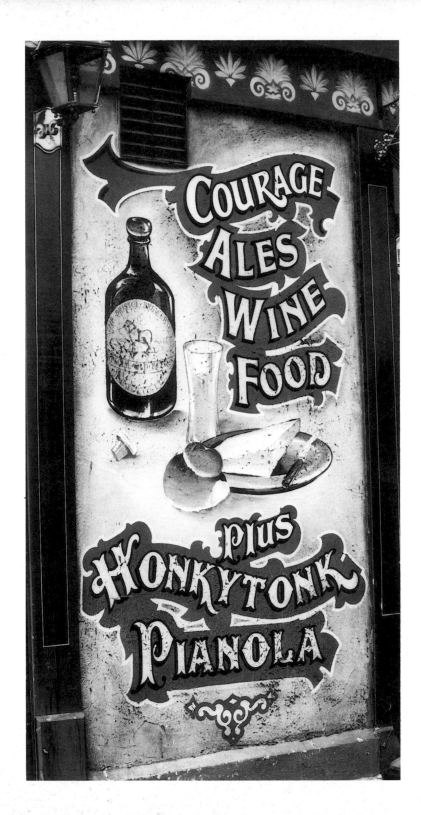

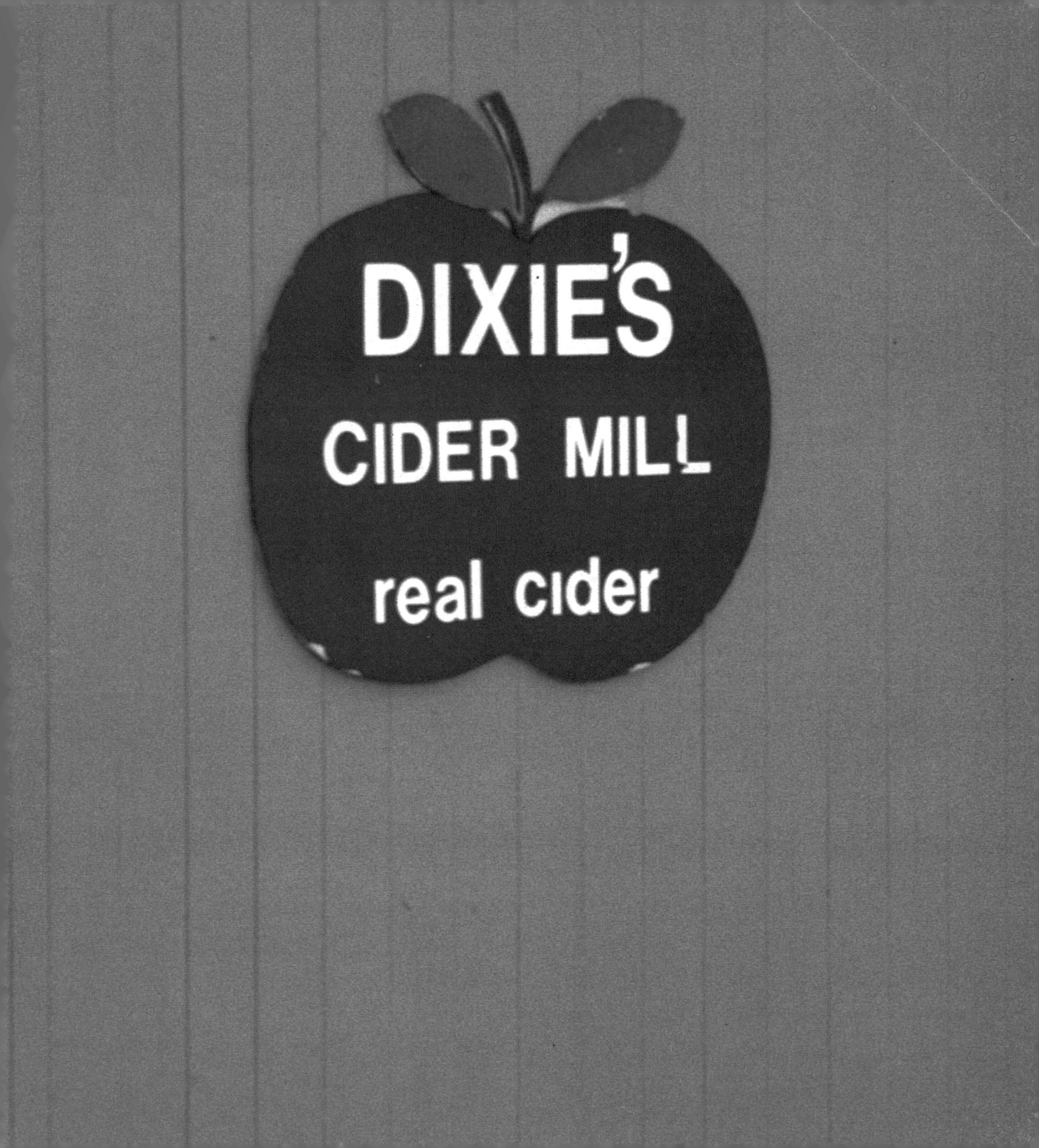
DIXIE'S
CIDER MILL
real cider

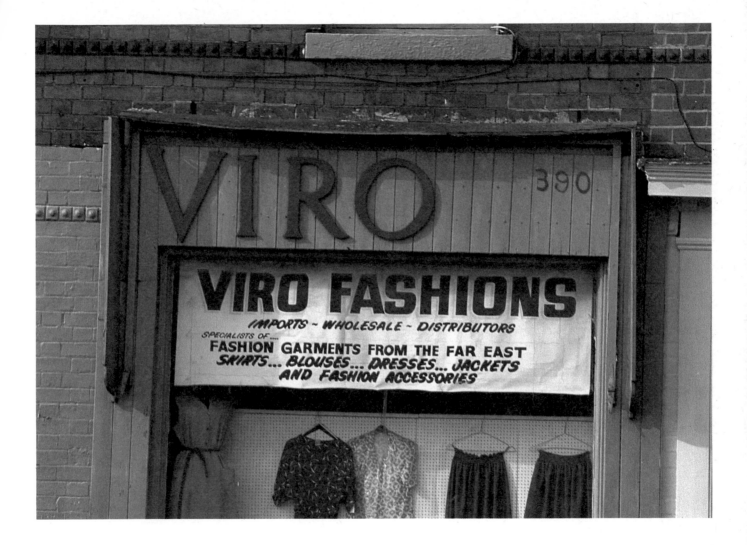

ANSWERS 3ᴰ.

VULCANIZING
BY **H.F.** THE
PROCESS

SLOTTED
ANGLE
SERVICES
Tel. 45510.

SON OF
WISHEE-WASHEE

SPLISHEE-SPLOSHEE
CLEANEE-KNICKEE
VELLEE-QUICKEE

*Collector's Corner*

# Index